Elegies & Devotions

Elegies & Devotions

Poems by

Thomas DeFreitas

Cover design by Shay Culligan
Cover image by Tommy Bond via Unsplash

ISBN: 978-1-63980-852-6

Kelsay Books
502 South 1040 East, A-119
American Fork, Utah 84003
Kelsaybooks.com

Acknowledgments

Thank you to the following publications, in which versions of these poems previously appeared:

Autumn Sky Poetry DAILY: Elegy VI in "A Garland for Jen" (as "Crowded Cambridge Buses")

Elegies I, II, III, VI, XII, and XIII appeared in *Longfellow, Tell Me* (Kelsay Books, 2022) under the following titles:
"For a Moment" (I)
"Stop All the Clocks" (II)
"Last Saturday" (III)
"Crowded Cambridge Buses" (VI)
"Requiescat" (XII)
"You Should Have Seen the Rain" (XIII)

Contents

A GARLAND FOR JEN

I

For a moment,
earlier,
I had the urge to call you up
and tell you
that you died today.

II

Let YouTube and Facebook go dark;
Let Frisbees be banned from JFK Park:
    Let pizza-parlors lose their dough,
    The grass-banked Charles dry up its flow.

Dive-bars on Causeway Street, close down.
Rose-petals, wither. Summer leaves, turn brown.
    Skies, grow sick as a grunge band's mood;
    Young buskers, pause and sit and brood.

Preacher, stuff your rant about sin.
Used car salesman, wipe off that grating grin.
    Glad-handing candidate, quit your *spiel*.
    My friend lies dead. Bow down and kneel.

I've thought of sending her a text.
But her fierce heart's stopped beating. Christ, what next?
    I've wept a Black Sea ten miles deep:
    There's nothing I can do but weep.

Her shoulder's cold: I cannot lean.
We won't chat on the phone till 2:15.
    Her eyes are locked against the sun:
    The days I laughed with her are done.

III

Last Saturday you died:
our sky was one great cloud;
hot rain pounded upon my path
from that saturate shroud.

Lavishly fell the tears
from heaven's widow-black,
but could not match this scalding flood
as I lament my lack:

the loss of your rare charm,
my fast immediate friend,
bound close in life, snatched far by death,
forever reverend.

My words falter and fail,
my voice cracks up and chokes.
Such a dear gift our thoughtless God
impulsively revokes!

Always you were the one
who made me smile and laugh:
I never thought that I would write
your midday epitaph.

So desperately I wish
that this truth were not true:
each morning I must wake and walk
through a world stripped of you.

Make me strong with your strength
for the time that I have left
that I might learn to bear the pain
of heaven's senseless theft.

From now on, let me live
so bravely and so right
that when my days are spent we shall,
two glad friends, reunite.

Jen, bless me from your place,
there, on the other side
of death's grim brink, where now you live
refreshed, beatified.

IV

I remember
that hot November day
77 degrees
the three of us

you and me and Debba

we sat in Sheila's booth
at the Arlington Diner
for midafternoon breakfast

omelets the size of Montana

when you drove up Mass Ave
you blew cigarette smoke
through the rolled-down window

the wind blew it back in

you nudged the gas pedal
with a flip-flopped foot

during the car ride
you and Debba
mentioned Murph
the 80-year-old fixture
of the Allston nooner

you called Murph
a mack daddy

*

our friendship
took root and flourished
as the months went by

if you saw I was getting
cranky on Facebook
you'd call me up
at 10 at night

talk to me kid
what's goin' on

I'd always thank you
you'd always shrug it off

it's what friends do
you'd do the same for me

*

the Easter before your last
I gave you
the Glenstal Book of Prayers
with the purple cover
and a book of Rosary stories

miracles and wonders

you gave me the preconciliar missal
half in French half in Latin
that had belonged to Sister Philomena
your beloved aunt

*

I can still see
the glow-in-the-dark Batman logo
on your black t-shirt
as you sat up in your hospital bed
chatting with visitors

At one point
I made bold to say
I just adore you

and you said *oh
right back atcha*

V

Surrounded by flowers
you lie in a sleep
from which nothing can rouse you:
black dress, modest silver cross
sideways on your necklace.

This past week,
a gauntlet of grief:
chest-racking sobs
five, six, seven times a day.

Adam played the violin for you:
Schubert's *Ave Maria.*

He played it at your wake on Thursday.
He played it at your Mass on Friday.

I bawled both times.

*

God stole you from us.

You were God's to begin with?

Well, then, God was a loan-shark
who forced us to pay you back
with the extortionate interest
of our entire heart.

Infallible Omnipotence
took your lovely flourishing womanlife
and dashed it against the rocks.

Oncology.
Chemotherapy.
Metastasis.

Compromised immunity.
No visitors.

Spiteful caprice.
Vicious whim.

How can I possibly
pray to Him?

VI

I won't sing a winsome ballad,
As my strings are all unstrung;
I'll forsake my merry mischief:
You were taken far too young.

I won't swim the English Channel;
I won't climb an Alpine peak—
Since you died, my hopes are rubble:
I've been crying for a week.

I won't lift a glass of Guinness;
I'll abstain from Maker's Mark:
I'll put down the gin martini
(No more cocktails after dark).

How I've searched for you in churches!
But despite my anguished prayer,
All I see are sculpted angels:
I can't find you anywhere.

August will collapse to autumn
With its nights of killing frost:
Faith would say that God has gained you;
I will weep for what I've lost.

Now I stumble through a city
Where the trace and trail of you
Evanesce to cherished memories
In my heart so bruised and blue.

You were sunlight, you were fire,
You were Holy Eucharist:
You were Irish Catholic Boston;
Yours, the blush-bright cheek I kissed.

In the spring, you had a backache,
Then they told you what it was,
And it stole you in the summer:
I ask why; there's no because.

I can't rouse you from your coffin;
I can't raise you from the dust:
I can't get your stopped pulse beating;
I protest because I must.

Can't you call me up or text me,
Speak some solace through the phone?
I ride crowded Cambridge buses,
But I'm horribly alone.

VII

A mere forty days   a hot-weather Lent
from your diagnosis
until your death

And every night   I pray for you

in my domestic chapel
where icons grace the walls

with holy cards of a hundred saints

in the wee corner of my apartment
where rosaries hang from thumbtacks

Each time I pray
grief warps your name
to sobs of incoherence

VIII

Over the buzz and welter of a Boston summer,
over the tense calm of three in the morning,
over the hum of an overworked air-conditioner,
over YouTube liturgies of incense and pomp,
over Instagram vespers with wimple and psalter,
over black coffee at the Thursday nooner,
over the Dropkick Murphys hollering "Tessie,"
over the People's Republic of Cambridge,
over Mount Pleasant headstones with Celtic crosses,
under the stringent mercies of Heaven,
through salt tears of fresh deprivation,
I tell memories like looped wooden beads;
I rehearse words of love and astonishment;
I pray *for* you: I pray *to* you.

IX

At your wake
your mom said to me
(her voice alive
with gentle evidence
of her native Ireland)
she was always there for people
always helping people

Fr Brian said the Mass
at St Columbkille's

Danny remembered you
in a eulogy boobytrapped
with affectionate jokes
and tearjerking memories

how badly you drove

how you cherished your recovery

how unfailingly kind you were
to anyone in need

we all had lunch
at the Stockyard afterwards
I sat with the eight pallbearers
(all of them women
all of them your friends)

and one inked-up fellow
describing how painful it was
to get a tattoo
of the Holy Name

Jesus was a nightmare

I have a heart-shaped vial
of Lourdes water
which Edward the ex-monk gave me

I'll never place it in your hands

we'll never make the trip
to Battery Street
in the North End
to visit the sprawling
brick-alley shrine
called All Saints Way

but I'll always remember the day we met
you and me and Debba
at the Arlington Diner

the holy reckless bright transfiguration
that knocked seven bells out of me

I'll listen to the soundtrack
of our friendship

we didn't really have
a specific playlist
but certain songs seem right

anything Celtic
anything Catholic
anything big and boisterous

U2's *Gloria*
Van Morrison's *Moondance*
Tantum Ergo Sacramentum
these are the days
of miracle and—

I can never deliver
the several million kisses
I had saved up
for the ground you walked on
and for the feet you walked with

X

You were sitting beside me on a small couch.
You were describing the death of a relative, how she
had been diagnosed with cancer, and was treated
with chemotherapy, but the chemo decimated
her immune system, and she died shortly thereafter.

I shook my head gently.

No, that's not what happened.
You had cancer, Jen. And you died.

You smiled at me. You could not contradict.

I woke up, hot with anguish.
One in the morning. I found a calendar
and calculated. Seventy-seven days
since that rainy Saturday.

With the knife of your death alive again in me,
I sobbed for an hour and keened your name
to angels and saints, to the bedroom ceiling.

And I was grateful.
Grateful for this unforgetting,
this remembrance of you—

my solace and strength, my refuge and rest.

XI

I introduced you
and my two
best friends

to my cousins
at Dad's wake
in March:

this is Heather,
my high-school
sweetheart;

this is Deborah,
my post-high-school
sweetheart;

and this is Jen—
she's just a sweetheart,
full stop!

Who knew, Jen,
that a mere
five months later

a lurking cancer
would claim you
and leave me

sobbing, blind,
raging, hurt,
who knew

that Fr Brian
who conducted

Dad's service

would do the same
for you,
who knew

that for weeks
after your death
I'd be walking

around Boston
and have to stop
and wail in alleyways,

who knew
that our friendship
during its third year

would become
(in the phrasing
of old prayerbooks)

ghostly,
who knew
that whenever

I'd talk to you
from now on,
I'd be addressing

your laminated
prayer card

XII

The face that made my cold heart melt
    Is scattered ash upon the plain;
The feet at which I should have knelt
    Will never walk this way again.

The heart that pulsed with love and rage
    Is dead as carved dates on a stone;
That voice, struck dumb in middle age
    That told me, *You are not alone.*

Those shining, fierce, compassionate eyes
    No longer laugh, no longer weep;
That mind—so mischievous, so wise!—
    Has slipped into perpetual sleep.

XIII

Jen, how it rained and rained the day you died.
Who would have thought the sky could weep so much?
It was as if the clouds had never cried,

had held cold centuries of tears inside
until the knife of grief began to cut.
Oh, how it rained and rained the day you died.

Hours passed. The downpour just would not subside;
gutters were gushing with a frantic flood:
it was as if the clouds had never cried.

A hot and angry jag. No one could hide
from this great soak and seethe, this drench and clutch.
It rained and kept on raining when you died.

Let there be light. Could Genesis have lied?
God's brightest joy! Too soon extinguished, crushed.
All the clouds cried as if they'd never cried.

I cursed the justice of the Crucified
who turned your strength and substance into dust.
It rained and wouldn't stop the day you died.
It was as if the clouds had never cried.

XIV

Jen, I haven't written to you
since—when? since my last dream of you?
since the last rain-drenched anniversary

of your death? Jen, beautiful bad-ass,
Irish-American fire-flower, how
my heart would dance at the merest

thought of you. You were with Danny,
and of course I accepted that. But
candidly I often wished we could have

been closer. I wish we had had more
than 33 months of lunches and meetings
to explore our friendship. I wish

we could have sat in a pizza-pad, gobbling
slice after slice, as I nattered about
my latest poem, and you told me stories

of the bad old days, when characters
you'd meet in dark places would call you
diabla blanca, or maybe you'd tell me

stories of Sister Philomena, your aunt
who helped the poor in San Antonio.
Jen, forthright speaker, always loyal

to Debba and Lisa and me, you were
deeply Catholic but no plastic saint
with a halo. You felt love and pain

and took them straight, no chaser,
Jen whose name to me is prayer—and
oh, listen to me ramble! and yet

I would keep speaking, if saying more
could conjure you back to earth for a few
more laughs, a few more bright-eyed smiles,

a hug when a hug was the only certain cure.
God damn the cancer that took you from us, Jen.
I miss you inconsolably, you earthy woman,

maculate and boisterous, who blessed
any soul in need, who cursed any jerk,
who smoked and drove not smoothly

but with fierce determination,
who knew, who must have known,
how deeply I cherished you:

dearest, kindest, take-no-bullshit Jen.

XV

It rains cold rain
in the sixth winter
of a world still sore
from the loss of you.

And now, thunder!
Wow! Haven't heard
a crack like that
since last summer.

Sky's a dark river
roiling with all manner
of gripe and grief
and perturbance.

Somehow, I'm calm
finding this storm
an odd reassurance
that all will be well.

WHERE NO WATER IS

i am zaccheaus
fumbling up the sycamore
to catch a glimpse

i am the leper
flinging my corruption
onto the healer's mercy

i am the woman at the well
parched at high noon
as a dry and barren land
where no water is

i am the psalmist
grief dims my eyes

my beauty is gone
for very trouble

i am pope francis
kneeling to wash
the feet of inmates
on maundy thursday

i am a prisoner of sin
a mendicant of mercy
begging for blessings
greedy for grace

i am mary of bethany

and jesus rides the number 15 bus
in the heartadown dudley

smiling unsmiling
radiant and weary
brown and black faces
of the sweet lord christ

domine non sum dignus

but only say the word
and my soul shall be healed

repentance says a friend
does not wear a long face

as it is the freedom
to rejoice

*

it is liberating to be abject
it is exaltation to be humble
it is resurrection to be dust

*

the morning star
works in a bar
in the remnants of boston's west end

she gives light to those in darkness
she gives drink to the thirsty
she gives grace to the graceless

i wait in expectation of the lord

who does not incline
to hear my cry

a winter liturgy
in the roxbury convent

outside three degrees above zero
but warm in the modest
schoolhouse chapel

the old-shoe priest
father waldron
bald head bandaged
from recent surgery

octogenarian sisters
of the blessed sacrament
mary matthias among them
praying over the sound
of the hissing radiator

on a table in the back of the chapel
a beat-up paperback
by jesuit william barry
god and you

fewer than a dozen in attendance
and it was years ago

but i dared to believe
that this little mass
was changing the world

dare we hope
in a god
who loves us
not *in spite of*
but *because*

*

can our eyes discern
in love's humiliation
the delicate harbingers
of something called glory

can our soul perceive
in love's destitution
any bud any spear of grass
any sign of resurrection

my lord my god
you cannot be
that white-bearded cartoon

my lord my god
are you the love
that religion seems to forbid

my lord my god
can you restore
all that you have taken away

my lord my god
do you reside on high in the clouds
or among bricks and dust

my lord my god
behold your faithful servant
beneath a heap of rubble

my lord my god
who you do think you are
treating me this way

my lord my god
my heart cannot rest in you
you have given my soul no peace

my lord my god
you are the cruel fate
to which i am condemned

my lord my god
you are the cross
on which i hang

About the Author

Thomas DeFreitas was born in Boston, was educated at the Boston Latin School, and attended the University of Massachusetts (in Boston and in Amherst) for two years. His poems appear in *Autumn Sky Poetry Daily*, *Dappled Things*, *Ibbetson Street*, *Pensive*, *Plainsongs*, and elsewhere.

In April 2018, Thomas's poem "Chasing the Waves" was chosen by Arlington, Massachusetts Poet Laureate Cathie Desjardins to be part of the Talking Chair Project, an interactive poetry exhibit installed at the Robbins Library in Arlington. In the summer of 2019, "Detox" was chosen as an Award Poem by the editors of *Plainsongs.* In November 2024, "Grief" was nominated for a Pushcart Prize by the editor of *Autumn Sky Poetry Daily.*

Thomas's most recent full-length collection, *Walking Between the Raindrops*, appeared in February 2025 under the Kelsay Books imprint. His previous titles, all published by Kelsay, include *Swift River Ballad* (2023), *Longfellow, Tell Me* (2022), and *Winter in Halifax* (2021).

Thomas rejoices to be a member of St James's Episcopal Church in Cambridge, Massachusetts. Since joining the parish in 2020, he has served as reader, hymnographer, presenter of a "living epistle," cantor in a virtual service, deanery delegate, writer of poems for special liturgical observances, and on one occasion, preacher of the Sunday sermon.

His website:
thomasdefreitas.me